Health Care Sharing Ministries

How Christians Are Revolutionizing Medical Cost and Care

Stephen R. Turley, Ph.D.

TURLEY TALKS

A New Conservative Age is Rising

www.TurleyTalks.com

Disclaimer: Health care is a highly personal issue and must be pursued in discussion with health care professionals. The information I provide is on an as-is basis. I make no representations as to accuracy, completeness, suitability, or validity of any information in this book and will not be liable for any errors, omissions, or delays in this information or any losses, injuries, or damages arising from its use.

Table of Contents

Introduction: Health Care on the Brink   7

Chapter 1 The Good Samaritan: A Christian Vision of Healing   15

Chapter 2 Economies of Grace: The Real Significance of Health Care Sharing Ministries   23

Chapter 3 Health Care Sharing: How to Opt-Out of Obamacare and Bless Fellow Christians   29

Chapter 4 Health Care Independence: The Self-Pay Patient   37

Chapter 5 Faith-Based Medical Sectors and the Future of Post-Secular Health Care   45

Conclusion: The Christian Health Care Revolution   53

Resources   57

About www.TurleyTalks.com   63

About the Author   65

INTRODUCTION

Health Care on the Brink

Health care is on the brink of monumental change. According to researchers Jeff Elton and Anne O'Riordan, changes in technology, competition, and economic transactions are disrupting the health care industry in a manner akin to the ways such processes disrupted Kodak and Polaroid in photography and Blockbuster video stores for home entertainment.[1] Indeed, the sweeping legislative reach and uncertainty and instability surrounding the politics of health care, particularly involving the Affordable Care Act (or more commonly known as Obamacare), means that everyone is affected by these changes, both doctor and patient, health insurers and health providers, lab technicians and app developers.

With all of the medical rearrangements and permutations arising, what has yet to catch up to these changes is the way

---

[1] *Healthcare Disrupted: Next Generation Business Models and Strategies* (Hoboken, NJ: John Wiley & Sons, 2016).

health care is *administered.* The advances in medical science have hardly entailed advances in medical administration and delivery mechanisms. The business models associated with health care today very often belong to a time gone by. You've of course seen the libraries of manila folders behind the receptionist's desk, and you may have noted, too, that computers only recently made their way into examination rooms. In fact, Elton and O'Riordan argue that health care providers are going to have to adopt new and dynamic ways in which health care is administered and practiced if they don't want to go the way of Blockbuster.

What this means is that the latest innovations in health care are not so much driven by medical and scientific advances as they are by improving the ways in which health care is *accessed, provided,* and *paid for.*[2] Elton and O'Riordan point to what they call an "Amazon effect" taking place among the general population, where streamlining ordering, manufacturing, and delivering practices and expectations are beginning to disrupt and replace traditional hospitals, retail pharmacies, and therapeutics distributors. Increasingly, consumers defer to online retail experiences where they can shop for the best options as displayed conveniently on their computer screens or iPhones. Thus, we are seeing the rise of what's called "telehealth," which involves "a collection of means or methods for enhancing health care, public health, and health education delivery and support using

---

[2] Lauren Phillips, "What Will Health Care Look Like in 5-15 Years?" http://www.hfma.org/Leadership/E-Bulletins/2015/April/What_Will_Health_Care_Look_Like_in_5-15_Years_/

telecommunications technologies."[3] Sharing and obtaining health information via mobile apps and video conferencing with a physician are revolutionizing the way health care is administered. An online chat with a physician anywhere in the world, at a fraction of the cost of visiting a medical facility, can result in a called-in prescription pick up. In an increasingly Amazon-calibrated world, the patient is more and more becoming a consumer.

These changes are making traditional health insurance practices not only out-of-date, but overly expensive and unnecessarily cumbersome and frustrating. It is not unusual for health-plans to require a $5,000 deductible, and this on top of constantly rising premiums.[4] Moreover, traditional health insurance puts patients at the mercy of insurers and government bureaucrats who know nothing about individual needs and circumstances. Their decision on what to pay for and what not to pay for may have an even bigger role in determining the health care you receive than you and your doctor.

In his study on self-paying patients, Sean Parnell recalls the nightmare scenario of a woman suffering from severe migraine headaches. Research found that Botox injections were highly effective in migraine headache prevention. She participated in a clinical trial and found the injections worked wonderfully. But the cost of $900 per injection at a rate of

---

[3] Aine Cryts, "Four Tech Trends in Healthcare in 2017," http://managedhealth careexecutive.modernmedicine.com/managed-health care-executive/news/four-tech-trends-health care-2017.

[4] Dan Morgan, "Most popular Obamacare plans cost average of 34 percent more for 2018," https://www.cnbc.com/2017/10/25/most-popular-obamacare-plans-cost-average-of-34-percent-more-for-2018.html.

about three to four times per year was not covered by her employer's health insurance. It turns out that the insurer needed a particular code filled out on the medical form, which her doctor failed to do. Each time she tried to refine and correct omissions and form discrepancies, she was told the same thing: we will not pay for this. After six months of migraines, thousands of dollars of bills, and hundreds of hours wasted with her doctor and her insurance company, the insurer finally relented and paid the bill, but only after the patient threatened to file a grievance with the state attorney general.[5]

Perhaps the saddest part in this whole scenario is just how unnecessary it all was. This woman was participating in a *new* medical procedure but was beholden to an *old* method of payment and access. It is time to begin to think of health care provision and payment in innovative ways akin to the innovations in our wider ordering, manufacturing, and delivering industries.

Christian Health Care Sharing

It is precisely here that I believe the church has the answer: *health care sharing ministries.* Health care sharing ministries are not health insurance; they are rather organizations wherein Christians join to share the burdens of medical expenses of fellow members. As I will show throughout this book, Christian health care sharing offers a powerful and dynamic alternative to health insurance that combines the innovations noted above: lower premiums (in the form of

---

[5] Sean Parnell, *The Self-Pay Patient: Affordable Healthcare Choices in the Age of Obamacare* (Alexandria, VA: Self-Pay Patient, LLC, 2014), 12-13.

what are called "shares"), minimal deductibles, and self-pay consumer-based discounts for medical needs and procedures. These ministries have been around for decades, and have paid for billions of dollars of health care expenses for hundreds of thousands of patients.[6]

But in addition to contributing to the innovative trends that are redefining the administration and payment of health care, Christian health care sharing ministries are offering a *biblical* and *holistic* vision of health. First, they refuse to pay for procedures covered by health insurance plans such as contraception, sterilization, and abortion.[7] Secondly, most health care sharing ministries require that their members be Christian and abstain from behaviors and lifestyles that entail significant health risks, such as sexual promiscuity, homosexuality, drug use, and excessive drinking. Thus, the holistic vision of health is a distinctively *moral* vision; rooted in biblical principles, health is viewed not solely as a medical issue, but fundamentally a moral one.

My family and I have been members of Samaritan Ministries for years, and we consider Samaritan to be one of the best gifts we ever received as a family. For example, my son Richard was recently rushed by ambulance to a nearby hospital for what appeared to be an acute case of appendicitis. After several hours of tests, by God's grace, it was determined that his appendix was fine and that the pain was benign. The

---

[6] Parnell, *Self-Pay Patient,* 25.

[7] The good news here is that many states are passing laws prohibiting private health insurance providers from abortion coverage. See Rebecca Grant, "Does Your Insurance Cover Abortion?" https://newrepublic.com/article/144793/insurance-cover-abortion.

bill for the ambulance, private hospital room, and numerous tests was over $6,000. However, because we came in as self-paying customers, the hospital cut the bill in half. When we submit the need to Samaritan, *we expect to get every penny back!* This is because of the discounts that we get as the result of being a self-pay patient; we often don't have to pay a deductible, *since the discount is the deductible!*

In the pages that follow, I want to inspire you to consider joining what I believe to be nothing less than a revolution in health care. We will explore why it is that the Christian faith provides the answers to the current disruptions in conventional health care business models and insurance protocols. Chapter one explores the "Parable of the Good Samaritan" and how it radically altered our historical conceptions of compassion and neighbor. Chapter two provides an overview of how the early church worked out their new understanding of grace and philanthropy in the founding of hospitals, orphanages, and shelters for the poor. Chapter three explores how health care sharing ministries are at the vanguard of changes in the medical industry, providing faithful alternatives to conventional health insurance.[8] In chapter four, we discover how Christian health care sharing ministries free us from the confines of health insurance and enable us to take charge of our own health care decisions as - *self-pay patients.* This practice alone dramatically reduces the cost of care, thereby making it increasingly available to more and more people. Chapter five looks ahead at the ways in

---

[8] Special thanks goes to Mike Miller of Samaritan Ministries for his valuable insights and suggestions for these subsequent chapters.

which Christians are contributing to the emergence of a post-secular medical industry. The conclusion summarizes our findings, with a resource section to help you take control over your own health care needs along with contributing to those of your brothers and sisters in Christ.

And so, as it turns out, the way forward in health care innovation involves embracing the past or, better, the timeless. The way of a humane and affordable health care is timeless precisely because it is *the* Way; a life rooted in Christ, in fellowship and communion with the people of God, a life of mutuality and love, as we together look forward to the one who comes with healing in his wings (Mal 4:2).

.

CHAPTER 1

The Good Samaritan:
A Christian Vision of Healing

I remember attending a seminar at Durham University in the U.K featuring the renowned British sociologist of religion, David Martin. When asked about the state of Christianity in Britain, he quipped that the Christian faith had basically come down to two stories in the British imagination: "The Prodigal Son" and "The Good Samaritan." That was basically the extent of British familiarity with biblical Christianity.

As unfortunate as that might come across, Martin made another remark that made an indelible impression on me: he noted that Britain's socialist health care system was explicitly based on the Good Samaritan parable. I was struck by the irony that so-called universal health coverage has its roots in the very biblical Christianity that so much of the British population was increasingly unaware of. And while I vociferously demure from this statist outworking, I do believe it is incumbent on Christians to appreciate just how much the assumptions and practices of our modern health care industries throughout the West originally centered on the life-giving ministry of Christ and his church.

To that end, I want to offer a deep reading of "The Good Samaritan," and then, in the next chapter, explore briefly how biblical passages such as this contributed to nothing less than a total reimagining of Greco-Roman assumptions about the human person, health, and disease in distinctively Christian ways.

At one level, the parable is easy enough to grasp. A legal scholar asks Jesus what is required for one to inherit eternal life. Jesus in turn asks the scholar how he reads the Law. The legal expert recites two verses from the Law: "You shall love the Lord your God with all your heart and with all your soul and with all your strength and with all your mind (Deut 6:5), and your neighbor as yourself (Lev 19:18)." Jesus commends him, but the legal scholar presses on: "And who is my neighbor?"

It is important to recognize that Jesus does not answer the lawyer's question by referencing the Hebrew equivalent of Webster's Dictionary! Instead, he tells a story; and I think this is very significant regarding the nature of our humanity. I often ask my students: If you wanted to better understand what marriage is all about, would that inquiry be better answered by reading a Wikipedia article or by watching the first seven minutes of the Pixar animated film, *Up*? Of course, the latter they say, and that is because we were created not only to learn through stories but to actually participate in one, the grand biblical narrative of God's redemption of the world in Christ.

And so, Jesus tells a story:

> A man was going down from Jerusalem to Jericho, and he fell among robbers, who stripped him and beat him and departed, leaving him half dead. Now by chance a priest was going down that road, and when he saw him he passed by on the other side. So likewise a Levite, when he came to the place and saw him, passed by on the other side. But a Samaritan, as he journeyed, came to where he was, and when he saw him, he had compassion. He went to him and bound up his wounds, pouring on oil and wine. Then he set him on his own animal and brought him to an inn and took care of him. And the next day he took out two denarii and gave them to the innkeeper, saying, "Take care of him, and whatever more you spend, I will repay you when I come back." Which of these three, do you think, proved to be a neighbor to the man who fell among the robbers?" He said, "The one who showed him mercy." And Jesus said to him, "You go, and do likewise." (Luke 10:30-37, English Standard Version)

Modern readers can often overlook how shocking such a story would have been to its original Jewish audience. Biblical scholars have long recognized the historical enmity that existed between Jews and Samaritans in Jesus' day. N.T. Wright comments:

When Jesus told the story of the Good Samaritan, he did so deliberately to shock his audience.... Like so many of Jesus' brilliant stories, it operates at several levels. At the simplest level, of course, it is a spectacular invitation to a life of self-giving love, love in action, love that's prepared to roll up its sleeves and help no matter what it takes ... But at the next level down, it's a story designed to split open the worldview of its hearers and let in a shaft of new and unexpected light. Instead of the closed world of Jesus' hearers, in which only their own kith and kin were properly to be counted as neighbours, Jesus demands that they recognise that even the hated and feared Samaritan is to be seen as a neighbour.[9]

This antipathy between Jew and Samaritan provides an important insight into the rationale for a distinctively Christian approach to healing and welfare. The ancient world tended to define philanthropy and compassion in terms of kinship relations; if one was outside of such relationships, then there was little in the ancient worldview to justify any kind of obligation in the face of human need. As Bishop Wright makes clear, "The Good Samaritan" turns that worldview upside down: we are obliged to maintain the welfare of the entire human race as a single family and unified kin.

---

[9] "The Road to New Creation," http://ntwrightpage.com/2016/03/30/the-road-to-new-creation/.

But the early church fathers read this parable at an even deeper level. Ambrose recognized that there is a strange irony to the lawyer's answer regarding the twin imperatives of loving God and loving neighbor: the irony is that the very fulfillment of those twin commandments is standing right in front of the lawyer! As God became man, uniting the two natures in infinite love, the Incarnation is precisely that event that fulfills the whole of the Law. The parable, then, goes on to show us precisely how Jesus himself is that fulfillment.

The man who is travelling from Jerusalem to Jericho is often interpreted by the Church Fathers as Adam, the representative of the whole human race. He leaves Paradise (Jerusalem) and is exiled into the world (Jericho). The robbers signify the demonic forces that seek to destroy humanity, stripping him of his dignity and divine worth.

Origen of Alexandria discerned that the priest who passes by the beaten man represents the Law. We should not be too hard on the priest in the story; we can assume that the priest did not know if the man was dead and, if he was, then the priest would have contracted corpse contamination which would have interfered with his Temple duties.[10] So, too, the Levite, who Origen sees as representing the Prophets. Both the Law and the Prophets are powerless to help Adam who has come under the power of Satan and the demons. If there is going to be help, it must come from outside of this world.

---

[10] See Kenneth E. Bailey, *Jesus Through Middle Eastern Eyes: Cultural Studies in the Gospels* (Downers Grove, IL: InterVarsity Press, 2008), 292-3.

And so, we are introduced to the Samaritan. The Samaritan in a sense comes wholly outside of the legal and prophetic life of Israel, and brings a healing that cannot be found in this world. Hence the Samaritan is interpreted as Christ coming to Adam. He bandages his wounds (the 'wounds' are often read as 'sins') with oil and wine. Ancient Christian baptism often included the administration of *chrism* or holy oil representing the Holy Spirit on the initiate, and baptism was of course followed by the cup of communion. Further, the Samaritan brought the man to an inn where he further took care of him. This inn is interpreted as the church which, on the occasion of the Samaritan departing, has been entrusted to care for the man with two coins which, in Ambrose's interpretation, represent "the two Testaments that contain revealed within them the image of the eternal King, at the price of whose wounds we are healed."[11] And of course, this church will be entrusted with healing the man until the time the Samaritan returns.

Thus, Augustine sees each Christian participating in the salvation wrought by the Samaritan:

> Robbers left you half-dead on the road, but you have been found lying there by the passing and kindly Samaritan. Wine and oil have been poured on you. You have received the sacrament of the only-begotten Son. You have been lifted onto his mule. You have believed that Christ became flesh. You have been brought to the

---

[11] Cited in Arthur A. Just, *Luke* in *Ancient Christian Commentary on Scripture III* (Downers Grove, IL: InterVarsity Press, 2003), 180.

inn, and you are being cured in the church.[12]

The Good Samaritan rightfully occupies a central place in the Christian imagination. It is a timeless and beautiful story of reconciliation, healing, and redemption. But more than that, it is the story of Christ and the salvation of the entire cosmos in his own transformative life, death, and resurrection. Christ himself is the fulfillment of the love of God and the love of neighbor and the redemption of the world.

As such, Christ-followers from the very beginning were characterized by their philanthropic acts of grace and mercy, so much so, that Christian compassion could have been considered the *fifth* mark of the church (i.e. "I believe in one, holy, catholic, apostolic, and *philanthropic* church").[13] A fraternal order of believers rooted in Christ and extending beyond any single race, kin, or ethnicity would provide the key frame of reference by which a new age of gift and gratitude would dawn throughout the Mediterranean world and beyond.

---

[12] Cited in Just, *Luke*, 180.

[13] John A. McGuckin, "Embodying the New Society: The Byzantine Christian Instinct of Philanthropy," in Matthew Pereira, ed., *Philanthropy and Social Compassion in Eastern Orthodox Tradition* (New York: Theotokos, 2010), 50-71.

CHAPTER 2

Economies of Grace: The Real Significance of Health Care Sharing Ministries

Health care sharing ministries have a long history in Christian civilization and practice. Given the healing ministry of Jesus and parables such as "The Good Samaritan," it is no surprise that philanthropy has been central to Christian life and mission since its beginning. By the sixth-century, health care, particularly in the forms of hospitals, leprosaria (hospitals for the treatment of leprosy), orphanages, geriatric homes, and food-relief centers, became a characteristic part of the church's ministry.

Nevertheless, there remain detractors regarding the rise of health care sharing ministries. In an article published in *The New York Times* earlier this year entitled "Onward, Christian Health Care?" Professor Molly Worthen questions the resemblance of Christian health care sharing ministries to their supposed biblical and church precedents. She notes (strangely) that Jesus' healing ministry "didn't take pre-existing conditions into account," and that the early church "offered aid to nonbelievers." She goes on to observe that the real precursors to health care sharing ministries are the mutual aid societies of the nineteenth- and early twentieth-centuries. These societies provided relief from medical expenses and lost wages while stressing a stringent ethical code of conduct. Similarly, contemporary Christian health care sharing requires members to "live by biblical standards," which is integral to the formation of a distinctively Christian community.

Though appreciative of health care sharing ministries, Prof. Worthen remains skeptical. For her, the "great insight" of FDR's New Deal was its exposing the fallacious notions that local communities and free markets can solve society's problems. She thus defers to the Affordable Care Act, which is portrayed as the latest chapter of the New Deal's commitment to grant "a basic level of economic security to people excluded by the market or mutual aid."

I find a number of misconceptions in Prof. Worthen's piece, which will serve to help illuminate the real significance of health care sharing.

First, her implied assertion that the early church provided health care to nonbelievers is historically inaccurate and reductionist. In his important book, *From Monastery to Hospital: Christian Monasticism and the Transformation of Health Care in Late Antiquity,* Andrew T. Crislip documents how the revolution of health care in the fourth- and fifth-centuries actually blossomed out of the exclusive medicinal practices of Christian monasteries in secluded desert communities. In fact, this seclusion was essential to the reformation of health care, since such care developed as the necessary consequence of the monk's renunciation of the relationships constitutive of traditional society. The monastery thus provided surrogate services for a very specific group of believers, those without home or kin to take care of their physical needs.

Moreover, Prof. Worthen overlooks the fact that the extension of health care by Christians to non-believers involved nothing less than a totalizing reimagining of health and disease in Greco-Roman society. For example, the church overcame successfully the ancient conception of the ubiquity and irreversibility of Fate, which for centuries had deterred charity in response to sickness and wretchedness, since such compassion could be interpreted as interfering with the punishment of the gods. Instead, the church proclaimed a Trinitarian theology manifested in the "cursed" form of the crucified one, which essentially did away with the ancient stigmatization of sickness. Furthermore, while Greek social care was limited to kinship ties, the Christian expansion of universal kinship in Christ entailed an expansion of universal social compassion. Hence, by the fourth-century, a vast network of welfare services developed through the auspices of the church. Figures such as Ephraim the Syrian and Basil the Great established hospitals for those ravaged by plagues or leprosy. St. Benedict made caring for the sick a priority for his developing monastic order, and by the twelfth-century the Benedictines had established over 2,000 hospitals in Western

Christendom. Moreover, all of the hospitals were centers for food, clothing, and shelter for the poor, widows, and orphans.

Thus, in rooting Christian health care sharing ministries in the mutual aid societies of the nineteenth- and early twentieth-centuries, Prof. Worthen fails to mention that such societies were themselves constituents of centuries of Christian social recalibrations and the concomitant reinterpretation of sickness and disease. What secular academics so often overlook is that their concern for universal health coverage is itself a value specific to the Christian faith. It is the advent of Christianity that reimagined the human race as a universal fraternity organically unified in the First Adam and called to a redemptive life blossoming forth from the Second Adam. Philanthropic care was considered central to this salvific call. One might ask Prof. Worthen, wherein is such a salvific call in the Affordable Care Act?

As to Prof. Worthen's deference to state-run health care, she disregards how the modern state increasingly transformed the calculus inherent in the church's conception of health care from that constituted by charity and virtue to entitlement and taxation. As the executive mandate on contraception in the Affordable Care Act indicates, this redefinition changes the very concept of humanity itself: while the cultivation of love and virtue was at the heart of the Christian social order, litigation and regulation constitute the life blood of the modern secular welfare state. And as a mechanistic humanism replaces sanctity and virtue, institutions dependent on such sanctity and virtue, such as the family, begin to lose their relevance. It is in such a world that abortion and contraception appear highly plausible and desirable, thus rendering the executive mandate on contraception in the Affordable Care Act fairly predictable.

And so, Christian health care sharing provides more than just a way in which the church can give witness to what it means to be a shared lifeworld of mutuality and service. In continuity with centuries of philanthropic redefinitions and care, such ministries indeed provide a different and redeemed way of being human, where Christians across the nation enact an economy of grace serviced by gift and gratitude, in stark contrast to the dominant secular economy of entitlement and taxation. It is the church, not the secular state, that provides the frames of reference that awaken a truly charitable and humane society, one that calls all to the redemptive healing of the New Adam, who came that we might have life and have it abundantly (John 10:10).

CHAPTER 3

Health Care Sharing: How to Opt-Out of Obamacare and Bless Fellow Christians

As we noted above, health care is on the brink of massive changes. The ways in which health care is *accessed*, *provided*, and *paid for* have yet to catch up to the medical, technological, and scientific advances that are more and more defining modern medicine. We noted earlier an "Amazon effect" taking place among the general population, where streamlining ordering, manufacturing, and delivering practices and expectations are beginning to disrupt and replace traditional hospitals, retail pharmacies, and therapeutics distributors.

Christians are in fact at the vanguard of these changes and revolutionizing the way health care is accessed, provided, and paid for through health care sharing organizations. Now these organizations were barely on the map before the Affordable Care Act. But since the ACA or Obamacare was passed, tens of thousands of people have looked for alternatives to the constant spike in health insurance premiums and the ever-increasing deductibles. And many have found such an alternative in health care sharing organizations such as Samaritan Ministries, Christian Health Care, Medi-Share, and Liberty Health Share. In fact, the health care sharing ministry to which I belong, Samaritan Ministries, served 1,000 households back in 1997; as of August 2017, it serves nearly 70,000 households comprised of over a quarter of a million people.[14] In fact, since the passage of Obamacare, total membership in health care sharing ministries has skyrocketed to over a million participants.[15]

Health care sharing is not insurance, but because of its faithful fulfillment in sharing medical expenses, congress specifically and explicitly exempted health care sharing ministry members from the ACA tax penalty for being uninsured.[16] Instead, Christians join together to share in each other's medical expenses in fulfillment of Galatians 6:2: "Bear ye one another's burdens, and so fulfil the law of Christ." Each month, members receive a letter about another member's medical needs and expenses, and then send their share

---

[14] https://samaritanministries.org/help/faq.

[15] As of February 2017. Kate Shellnutt estimates the number at 625,000. See Kate Shellnutt, "Bearing Burdens After Obamacare: The Future of Christian Health care Sharing," http://www.christianitytoday.com/ct/2017/february-web-only/future-of-christian-health care-ministries-after-obamacare.html.

[16] "Health Care Sharing Ministry Exemptions," https://obamacarefacts.com/health care-sharing-ministry-exemptions/.

(instead of sending a premium to a health insurance company) directly to that member, along with notes of prayer and encouragement. For Samaritan, administrative services are paid for by each member sending one share per year to the Samaritan office.

The shares are often dramatically less expensive than health insurance premiums. According to Parnell, a 25-year old individual willing to be personally responsible for $2,500 in medical expenses will end up paying just over $100 a month through any of the four ministries noted above. A family of four with a 52-year old as its oldest member would pay around $480.[17] At Samaritan, medical needs up to $300 are the responsibility of the patient. Costs between $300 and $250,000 are shared by the other members. Medical expenses that exceed $250,000 are shared through another Samaritan ministry called Save to Share™.[18] Any rate increase requires a super-majority vote among members.

Among the medical needs shared are illnesses or injuries requiring visits to medical doctors, emergency rooms, and testing facilities, as associated with cancer treatments, maternity costs, diabetes, surgeries, and the like. What are not shared are illnesses related to behaviors considered inconsistent with biblical standards, such as sexual promiscuity, homosexuality, drunkenness, and drug addiction. These ministries also refuse to have anything to do with abortion, sterilization, contraception, and transgenderism. In this sense, Christian health care sharing

---

[17] Parnell, *Self-Pay Patient,* 25.
[18] https://samaritanministries.org/help/faq.

involves a highly *moral* conception of health care, wherein the whole person is dedicated to God and the salvific vision of health that he alone provides. To that end, Samaritan requires each member to be a practicing Christian, along with a signature from his or her pastor affirming faithful church attendance every year when membership is renewed. Having said that, all four ministries listed above report that they have never failed to pay an eligible need.[19]

Now my family and I have been a part of Samaritans Ministries for a number of years, as have been several of my colleagues at the classical school at which I teach, along with a number of friends. This for me is not merely a good idea or interesting theory. Health care sharing ministries offer a fundamentally different paradigm than that of health insurance, and that paradigm shift involves the radically personal nature of health care sharing ministries as opposed to the radially depersonalized nature of health insurance. Health care sharing organizations are in effect virtual communities that encourage and support one another. When we submitted a need after my son, Richard, broke his foot, we received a number of cards addressed to Richard from Christians all across the country, encouraging him with assurances of prayer for a speedy recovery. I can't tell you how beautiful it was to share with my son the love of Christians he never even met. Through health care sharing, Christians come together in a spirit of mutuality in sharing one another's costs and burdens. Of course, the Amish and many Mennonites have been doing this for decades.

---

[19] Parnell, *Single-Pay Patient,* 26.

This stands in such stark contrast to the impersonal nature of health insurance, where payment is made almost anonymously irrespective of the patient and the patient's needs. Sean Parnell refers to the predominant health care delivery and payment system as *bureaucratic medicine.*[20] Bureaucratic medicine involves third parties who know little about the patient's needs and circumstances, have little to no medical training to inform their understanding of the diagnosis, but have an inordinate influence and determination in what kind of health care you receive. With health insurance, the issue generally boils down to the cost of procedures and little more. Against the backdrop of Christian health care sharing, health insurance can be seen as a highly dehumanizing way of financing medical expenses. Moreover, this thoroughly secular approach to health care administration and payment often supports behavior that contradicts biblical ethics, such as sexually transmitted diseases[21] and abortion.[22] In many ways, secular health insurance contradicts the entire conception of health care as envisioned by Christians, who provided the original philanthropic foundations from which we derive much of our modern health care norms in the first place.

The personal nature of Christian health care sharing can be seen in how pre-existing conditions are treated. My own

---

[20] Parnell, *Single-Pay Patient,* 12.

[21] http://www.personalhealthinsurance.com/does-health-insurance-cover-std-testing/.

[22] Three states – California, New York, and Oregon – actually require insurance policies to cover abortion. See https://nwlc.org/resources/state-bans-insurance-coverage-abortion-endanger-women%E2%80%99s-health-and-take-health-benefits-away-women/.

health care sharing ministry, Samaritan, does not deny membership to anyone for health reasons. While needs from pre-existing conditions are not eligible for sharing under the monthly shares, they may be submitted as what is called a "special prayer need." These needs fall outside what's shared by the monthly shares, but are included in a month's share slip for voluntary giving above and beyond one's monthly share.[23]

The benefits of health care sharing ministries can extend to employers as well. Small to midsize employers can offer their employees the option of health care sharing as opposed to health insurance benefits. This is the arrangement that I'm currently enrolled in through my classical school. Employers can pay the monthly share for their employees, which for Samaritan is currently $160 for an individual and $405 for a family.[24] This of course represents a dramatic cost differential from health insurance. According to the Kaiser Family Foundation/Health Research & Educational Trust 2014 Employer Health Benefits Survey, the average annual health insurance premium for a family is $16,843, and for individuals $6,025.[25] What's essential for employees to understand is that small firms are increasingly unable to afford health coverage. A recent study by the Bureau of Labor Statistics found that less than 60 percent of workers at companies with less than

---

[23] https://samaritanministries.org/blog/hcsm-myth-9-people-with-pre-existing-conditions-are-turned-away.
[24] Elaine Pofeldt, "5 smart ways small firms can slash health-care costs," https://www.cnbc.com/2015/01/08/5-smart-ways-small-firms-can-slash-health-care-costs.html.
[25] https://www.kff.org/report-section/ehbs-2014-summary-of-findings/.

100 employees had access to health care through their employers.[26]

Whether we like it or not, health care is on the brink of major changes in how it is accessed, administered, and paid for. The wonderful news is that Christians are at the vanguard of this change. Through health care sharing organizations and networks, faithful believers are tapping into social and economic dynamics where these changes are working for the *benefit* of their members, not only enabling them to opt-out of the current bureaucratic medical system, but actually thrive in doing so. The days of rising health insurance costs, red tape, and frustrations are over. Christians have a better way.

---

[26] https://www.bls.gov/news.release/ebs2.nr0.htm.

CHAPTER 4

Health Care Independence: The Self-Pay Patient

One of the most important contributions of Christian health care sharing ministries to our current health care system is how it resolves the problem of ever increasing medical costs. The average individual health care premiums have actually gone up 99 percent since 2013, and family premiums have increased a whopping 140 percent![27]

Christian health care sharing offers a vibrant and cost-effective alternative: *the self-pay patient.* By opting-out of health insurance and third-party bureaucracies, health care

---

[27] https://news.ehealthinsurance.com/news/average-individual-health-insurance-premiums-increased-99-since-2013-the-year-before-obamacare-family-premiums-increased-140-according-to-ehealth-com-shopping-data.

sharing ministries put the control over one's health care back into the hands of the patient.

This trend was the subject of a well-researched book published in 2014 by Sean Parnell entitled *The Self-Pay Patient: Affordable Healthcare Choices in the Age of Obamacare.* It's an important book that I would recommend as a supplement to this one. In just over 100 pages, he helpfully details a treasure-trove of affordable care options outside of conventional insurance. In this chapter, I will provide a summary of what becoming a self-pay patient involves and how it dramatically lowers the cost of health care.

We noted above the advent of what scholars are calling the "Amazon effect," which involves the ways in which traditional business models are impacted and altered by the digital marketplace and its effects on our consuming practices and habits. Health care, like any other industry, is being radically altered by these social and economic changes.

One of the most significant changes to the ways in which health care is accessed and paid for is through the advent of the *self-pay patient*. Simply put, self-pay patients opt-out of health insurance and pay health care providers directly for their services. This enables the patient and the provider to agree on a price amicable for both parties. Self-pay arrangements encourage competitive pricing up-front, which in turn prompts a willingness among providers to provide competitive discounts. The self-pay patient fits well with one of the major changes going on in health care, which is the advent of "value-based reimbursement," also known as "pay-for-performance," where compensation is directly linked to outcome-based services. Because health care is becoming increasingly consumer based, health care providers need to provide competitive services that focus on the overall quality of care they provide.[28]

The savings benefits from such a paradigm shift are significant. *The Wall Street Journal* recently published an article entitled: "How to Cut Your Health-Care Bill: Pay Cash." The article goes on to demonstrate that an increasingly consumer-driven health care system, where patients shop for the best deal, involves more and more hospitals, imaging centers, and pharmacies giving deep discount incentives for the consumer to pay cash. Not so long ago, self-pay patients were actually charged a higher rate; now, patients paying in cash often get far better deals than their insurers can negotiate for them. Resources such as MediBid and Healthcare Bluebook enable patients to solicit bids for services and find the best deal offered by providers respectively.[29] Conversely, hospitals have been actively seeking higher rates from insurers to make up for losses on other patients, the costs of which are passed on to the plan members. This accounts for the seemingly ever soaring high deductibles.

Research from Athena Health determined that patient-pay

---

[28] http://www.mckesson.com/population-health-management/population-health/know-the-challenges/.
[29] Both of these resources are available to Samaritan members for free.

now represents 20 percent of provider revenue.[30] Of interest is how high-deductible health plans are driving the patient pay trend. Only a million Americans had high-deductible health plans in 2005, this number jumped to nearly 20 million in 2014, and estimates project 40 million by 2018. What this means is that even the insured are becoming more and more self-pay patients. Indeed, hospitals report a 10 percent increase in self-pay patients over the last five years.

As such, online resources are emerging to help patients not only locate doctors who receive cash-based reimbursement, but also competitive pricing for various procedures. Resources such as Clearhealthcosts.com publish hard-to-find health care prices for consumers. With a quick trip to their site, you can find hospitals that perform MRI's for upwards of $2,000 versus clinics that can perform the same procedure for just $700.

The Amazon effect has also rendered the brick-and-mortar hospital increasingly superfluous. Today, there are over 10,000 clinic locations across the nation, offering patients convenient and cost-effective options and resources to meet their health care needs.[31] In fact, the growth and offerings of urgent care clinics are such that they are on the verge of covering as much as 30 percent of emergency room visits.

---

[30] See Doug Johnson, "New Research Examines Self-Pay Patients and the Changing Health care Industry," https://www.insidearm.com/news/00042377-new-research-examines-self-pay-and-changi/.
[31] Sara Heath, "Convenient, Cost-Effective Urgent Care Clinics on the Rise," https://patientengagementhit.com/news/convenient-cost-effective-urgent-care-clinics-on-the-rise.

One of the technological changes we noted above is the rise of what's called "telehealth" or "telemedicine," a virtual treatment which at one level involves direct medical consultation and diagnosis over the phone, skype, or email. But at another level, telehealth involves informative videos on diet and carbohydrate counting, apps estimating blood sugar levels and insulin needs, and online patient portals to see test results and request prescription refills.[32] Sharing and obtaining health information via mobile apps and video conferencing with a physician are revolutionizing the way health care is administered.

In terms of surgeries, there are a couple of options emerging. One involves outpatient or ambulatory surgery, which involve surgeries that don't require overnight hospital stays. A website known as Surgery Center Network provides a directory of ambulatory surgical centers for self-pay patients. These centers perform surgical procedures that are typically 45-60 percent less than the same procedure performed in a hospital, and sometimes as much as 80-90 percent less![33] As a bonus, patient surveys indicate a 90+ percent satisfaction with the care they received from ambulatory surgical centers.

A second option involves what's called *medical tourism.* You've heard of Canadians coming across the border to access a medical procedure without waiting in their socialist lines, or perhaps an American travelling to Costa Rica for an

---

[32] https://www.mayoclinic.org/healthy-lifestyle/consumer-health/in-depth/telehealth/art-20044878.

[33] http://selfpaypatient.com/2014/04/18/surgery-center-network-offers-low-cost-surgery-options/.

experimental procedure not offered here in the States. Regardless, medical tourism, the option to travel for medical procedures is becoming standard fare as part of an increasingly globalized health care industry. As such, resources such as North American Surgery provide networks of surgeons and health care providers at prices that are often 50 percent below U.S. hospital averages.

Advantages for the self-pay patient extend to prescription drugs as well. In addition to the discounts offered by Costco and Walmart, organizations such as Medsavers Pharmacy are emerging that offer cash-only transactions completely free of insurance companies. Because they are not subject to third party payer requirements to stock a certain amount of brand-name drugs, they lower their overhead costs and are thereby able to pass on the savings to their consumers.[34] They have a mail order program where they ship prescriptions within the states where the pharmacy or supplier is licensed. Moreover, Samaritan Ministries automatically enrolls all members in EnvisionRX, which often results in 50 percent reductions on the cost of their prescriptions.[35]

By transforming Americans into self-paying patients, Christin health care sharing is helping to lower health care costs across the board. Self-pay patients receive discounts from doctors who don't have to deal with insurance companies and receive payment directly, and shop around for the best price for visits,

---

[34] Yana Krinker, "Cash-Only Pharmacy Offers Savings on Medicines," http://selfpaypatient.com/2016/03/04/cash-only-pharmacy-offers-savings-on-medicines/.
[35] https://samaritanministries.org/why_samaritan/health_resources.

procedures, and prescriptions. And these two factors, discounts and price-shopping, significantly lower the price of health care and thereby widen its availability to more and more people.

In other words, Christian health care sharing is revolutionizing health care. It provides its own 'universal' mandate to share in one another's financial burdens but without the tax and entitlement mandates characteristic of de-personalized bureaucratic medicine. And, in so doing, health care sharing puts the patient in charge of his or her own health care, dramatically reducing its price and thereby making it more accessible. Christians are utilizing all of the technological advances in health care access and administration all the while fulfilling their mandate to care for one another's burdens. *This is the revolution of health care sharing ministries.*

CHAPTER 5

Faith-Based Medical Sectors and the Future of Post-Secular Health Care

Finally, it's not just in the area of health care sharing that Christians are leading the way in revolutionizing health care. There have been a number of very promising developments in the intersection between faith-based communities on the one hand and institutions of medicine and public health on the other, that I believe signal significant post-secular developments in the medical field.

As we noted above, one of the fundamental problems with modern secular medicine is its radically dehumanizing and depersonalized re-conception of the patient. Historically speaking, the patient and the disease are one, the disease is a part of the patient's personhood, the patient's story, his or her life and struggles. Today, we tend to engage in a process of objectification with regard to the disease; we treat the cancer or the medical condition as something that is wholly apart from the patient; the person doesn't need to be treated, only the condition, only the disease. The disease goes through a process of objectified depersonalization, any purpose or meaning of the disease is removed from the equation, and it simply becomes a biological or chemical agent that needs to be separated from the patient. In this sense, critics have noticed that modern medicine does not treat people but rather organisms.

However, it has not always been this way. Medical care under the guise of Christian faith-organizations has always preserved the sanctity and dignity of the human person. Indeed, it was the recognition of just such dignity and integrity that led to a mass health care revolution. We can very easily forget that there was simply no such thing as universal philanthropy before the rise of the Christian church, which of course involved the founding of hospitals. By the fourth-century, Christians established hospitals for those ravaged by plagues or leprosy. St. Benedict made caring for the sick a priority for his developing monastic order, and by the twelfth-century the Benedictines had established over 2,000 hospitals in Western Christendom.

This tradition of intersecting faith-based institutions and medical care continues into our own time, and it seems that conditions are ripe for a real renaissance in faith-based and post-secular health care. I'm drawing here from an insightful article by Jeff Levin on past, present, and possible partnerships between faith-based and medical sectors, where he notes that the intersection between faith-based institutions and medicine is quite multifaceted, and so he examines several points of intersection that appear very promising in the development of a thoroughly post-secular health care.[36]

For example, it may surprise you to find out that in the US, the church remains the primary owner and operator of non-profit health care facilities. In the US, non-profits make up over 80 percent of hospitals and the vast majority of these are sponsored by religious denominations. Just taking the Catholic Church as an example, their investment in health care services is absolutely staggering. The Catholic Church owns or is affiliated with 11 percent of all hospitals in the US and employs nearly 1 million workers. Three of the ten largest health care systems in the US are run by the Catholic Church, as are seven of the ten largest non-profit systems. Moreover, there are nearly 2,000 geriatric and nursing facilities, home care and hospice care services. While these services are intimately tied up with Medicare and Medicaid funding, Catholic affiliates nevertheless bear most of the burden for caring for their health care population.[37]

And in addition to all of this, they're very good at health care. There was a Reuters study in 2010 of 225 health systems in the US and it found that Catholic and other church-owned or affiliated systems were far more likely to provide higher

---

[36] Jeff Levin, "Partnerships between the faith-based and medical sectors: Implications for preventive medicine and public health," https://www.ncbi.nlm.nih.gov/pmc/articles/PMC4972923/.
[37] Gerald A. Arbuckle, *Humanizing Health care Reforms* (London and Philadelphia: Jessica Kingsley Publishers, 2013), 220-21.

quality of care and efficiency than secular and investor-owned for-profit health systems.[38]

Another area of intersection between faith-based industries and medicine is found in worldwide missions organizations. Today, tens of thousands of Christian medical missionaries are some of the primary medical, surgical, nursing, and dental providers on six different continents. They work together with NGOs or non-governmental organizations, academic institutions, and government agencies for the betterment of public health in underprivileged regions.

A very promising area of collaboration between church and medicine is community-based outreach to underserved populations. Today, there are partnerships between local health departments and faith-based organizations in every single region in the US to share resources to reach underprivileged communities and populations.

And the extraordinary power and relevance of faith-based organizations for medicinal care is catching the attention of the academy. More and more universities are featuring courses and research in 'Religion and Medicine' and establishing organizations such as the Institute for Spirituality and Health at the Texas Medical Center in Houston and the Institute for Public Health and Faith Collaborations at Emory University.

---

[38] Arbuckle, *Humanizing Health care,* 221.

But perhaps the most promising collaboration between faith-based institutions and medical care has been in the area of religious medical ethics, particularly in the role of advising and advocacy. This collaboration came into the foreground with the George W. Bush presidency and his establishment of the President's Council on Bioethics in 2001. Here we have conservative Christian medical and bioethicists advising the president on key bioethical and medical issues that shape national and public policy in highly human affirming ways. This is one of the most praiseworthy aspects of the advisory council, in that it brought some of the finest faith-based minds together to ask the essential questions of what it means to be human and the complexion of humanity's fundamental and most sacred values, those values that define and perpetuate our humanity, and how the medical industry can operate and flourish in accordance with those values.

This advisory role turned into advocacy and indeed at times quite hostile resistance during the Obama years and the challenges that Obamacare brought to those deeply concerned about the preservation of conservative medical ethics and a redemptive notion of what it means to be truly human. Virtually every major Christian denomination got involved with writing papers and mobilizing advocacy to preserve and protect the sanctity of human life and sexuality and religious freedom in the midst of Obama-era assaults.

Finally, we are seeing a fascinating interaction between the medical industry and federal faith-based initiatives. What the Bush-established Office of Faith-Based and Community Initiatives did is it offered the opportunity for faith-based organizations to compete alongside secular agencies to receive grants to provide for health care needs. You may be surprised to learn that as of today, faith-based offices are operative within a dozen federal cabinet departments, including the US Department of Health and Human Services.

Moreover, the concerns over the constitutionality of the partnership between the civil government and faith-based health care organizations appears to have waned, particularly in light of the Supreme Court's move away from the separationist paradigm that governed court decisions since 1940 to a more accomodationist paradigm that we saw with the recent Trinity Lutheran decision. The way it seems to be working is that if a church-based or faith-based organization is providing a service that is not specific to that organization, such as the administration of the sacraments, then that service most certainly qualifies for federal or state aid, since denying such aid on the grounds that the organization is religious is in fact religious discrimination. It does appear that this has become the default position of the Supreme Court for the foreseeable future, and promises significant partnership between church and state in all kinds of public endeavors, as in the case here of public health.

And so we are seeing more and more in a number of areas, such as the ownership and operation of hospitals and geriatric facilities, international missions organizations, academy based faith and health care institutions and research, faith-based advisory boards, and federally funded faith-based initiatives, that the days of secularized health care appear to be coming to an end. The church appears to be well-poised to help usher in a flourishing post-secular vision of the medical sector and, with it, a fully human affirming health care industry and service.

CONCLUSION

The Christian Health Care Revolution

Dramatic changes are taking place in the world of health care. Unfortunately, hospital business models and conventional health insurance policies and procedures have yet to catch up to the mass paradigm shift in how health care is accessed and paid for. As it turns out, Christian health care sharing organizations are leading the way in navigating these changes to the benefit of their members. Here's a summary of the ways in which Christians are revolutionizing health care:

The Philanthropic Mandate. As we learned from "The Good Samaritan," the Christian tradition of faith and life entails a divine mandate to bear the burdens of our brothers and sisters and thereby fulfill the law of Christ (Gal 6:2). As such, the Christian church has never needed a coerced mandate from the state to care for those in need.

The Self-Pay Patient. Perhaps the single biggest obstacle to health care access is *cost*. With the constant rise of premiums and procedures, combined with ever increasing deductibles, health care expenses are extending beyond the grasp of employers and employees. Christian health care sharing emancipates the patient from this debilitating spiral of health insurance and outdated health care delivery systems. It puts the patient in charge of his or her own health care, dramatically reducing its price and thereby making it more accessible. Christians are thus free to utilize all of the technological advances in health care access and administration.

Moral Medicine. Christian health care sharing involves a highly *moral* conception of health care, wherein the whole person is dedicated to God and the salvific vision of health that he alone provides. Health care sharing restores the notion of treating the whole person, not merely the disease, and thus requires its members to live lives in a manner glorifying to God. Unbiblical practices such as abortion are eliminated entirely from the purview of these ministries.

Post-Secular Health Care. In addition to health care sharing ministries, Christians are contributing to a thoroughly post-secular vision of the medical sector through the ownership and operation of hospitals and geriatric facilities, international missions organizations, academy-based faith and health care institutions and research, faith-based advisory boards, and federally funded faith-based initiatives. As the primary owner and operator of non-profit health care facilities throughout the US, the church continues to foster a fully human affirming health care industry and service.

Nevertheless, tens of millions of Christians remain stuck in the highly outmoded and passé forms of health care financing and administration. Their health care options remain confined by expensive insurance policies with escalating deductibles in a bureaucratic cycle of health insurers and delivery systems.

There is a new way, a better way, which turns out to be very old. Health care sharing stands in continuity with nearly two thousand years of Christian philanthropy, healing, and redemption. Bearing one another's burdens witnesses to the salvation of the entire cosmos in the transformative life, death, and resurrection of Christ. And as we come together to share in prayer needs and medical needs, we stand in continuity with centuries of faithful Christians who have together offered one another to the touch of the true healer, the Good Samaritan, the one in whom all things are made new (Rev 21:5).

RESOURCES[39]

Health Care Sharing Ministries

- Samaritan Ministries, www.samaritanministries.org, info@samaritanministries.org, (888) 268-4377
- Medi-Share, www.mychristiancare.org, info@mychristiancare.org, (800) 264-2562
- Christian Health care Ministries, www.chministries.org, (800) 791-6225
- Liberty HealthShare, www.libertyhealthshare.org, (855) 585-4237

Cash Friendly Doctors/Hospitals

- www.SimpleCare.com
- Association of American Physicians and Surgeons, https://aaps.wufoo.com/reports/m5p6z0/

Price Shopping

- www.PricePain.com
- www.SnapHealth.com
- www.DocCost.com
- www.DealWell.com

Urgent Care

- Urgent Care Association of America www.urgentcarecenter.org/findacenter.php

---

[39] More resources can be found in Parnell, *Self-Pay Patient* and his website: www.selfpaypatient.com.

- Find Urgent Care www.finurgentcare.com
- Urgent Care Guru www.urgentcareguru.com
- Health care 311 www.health care311.com

Telehealth Providers

- 1st Care MD, www.1stcallmd.com
- Teladoc, www.teladoc.com
- Ameridoc, www.ameridoc.com
- Consult a Doctor, www.consultadr.com
- CallMD, www.callmd.com
- DocDial, www.docdial.com

Ambulatory Surgical Centers

- Surgery Center Network,
  www.surgerycenternetwork.com

Medical Tourism

- North American Surgery,
  www.northamericansurgery.com **(866) 496-2764**
- MediBid, www.medibid.com (888) 855-6334
- Health Globe, www.myhealthglobe.com (800) 290-0197
- Medical Tourism Association,
  www.medicaltourismassociation.com

Imaging Services

- MRINet, www.mrinet.net
- Medtronic, www.medtronic.com
- American College of Radiology, www.acr.org
- Save On Medical, www.saveonmedical.com

Lab Services

- First Choice Labs USA, http://firstchoicelabsusa.com
- Laboratory Corporation of America, www.labcorp.com
- Quest Diagnostics, www. Questdiagnostics.com
- MD Lab Tests, http://gads.mdlabtests.com
- Save On Labs, www.saveonlabs.com
- EconoLabs, www.econolabs.com
- True Health Labs, www.truehealthlabs.com

Thank you again for purchasing this book!

I hope this book helped to awaken you to all the ways Christians are revolutionizing medical cost and care.

If you enjoyed this book, then I'd like to ask you for a favor: Would you be kind enough to leave a review for this book on Amazon? I would so greatly appreciate it!

Thank you so much, and may God richly bless you!

Steve Turley

www.turleytalks.com

Check Out My Other Books

Below you'll find some of my other popular books that are popular on Amazon. Simply go to the links below to check them out. Alternatively, you can visit my author page on Amazon to see my other works.

- *Movies and the Moral Imagination: Finding Paradise in Films*
  https://www.amazon.com/Movies-Moral-Imagination-classical-discernment-ebook/dp/B0774T7M12/
- *Classical vs. Modern Education: A Vision from C.S. Lewis*
  https://www.amazon.com/Classical-vs-Modern-Education-Homeschooling-ebook/dp/B0762Q387L/
- *Stressed Out: Learn How an Ancient Christian Practice Can Relieve Stress and Overcome Anxiety*
  https://www.amazon.com/Stressed-Out-Christian-Practice-management-ebook/dp/B076GDQZMC/
- *Awakening Wonder: A Classical Guide to Truth, Goodness, and Beauty*
  https://www.amazon.com/Awakening-Wonder-Classical-Goodness-Education/dp/1600512658/
- *Worldview Guide for* A Christmas Carol
  https://www.amazon.com/Worldview-Guide-Christmas-Classics-Literature/dp/1944503862/
- *The Ritualized Revelation of the Messianic Age: Washings and Meals in Galatians and 1 Corinthians*
  https://www.amazon.com/Ritualized-Revelation-Messianic-Age-Corinthians/dp/056766385X/

If the links do not work, for whatever reason, you can simply search for these titles on the Amazon website to find them.

About www.TurleyTalks.com

Are we seeing the revitalization of Christian civilization?

For decades, the world has been dominated by a process known as globalization, an economic and political system that hollows out and erodes a culture's traditions, customs, and religions, all the while conditioning populations to rely on the expertise of a tiny class of technocrats for every aspect of their social and economic lives.

Until now.

All over the world, there's been a massive blowback against the anti-cultural processes of globalization and its secular aristocracy. From Russia to Europe and now in the U.S., citizens are rising up and reasserting their religion, culture, and nation as mechanisms of resistance against the dehumanizing tendencies of secularism and globalism.

And it's just the beginning.

The secular world is at its brink, and a new traditionalist age is rising.

Join me each week as we examine these worldwide trends, discover answers to today's toughest challenges, and together learn to live in the present in light of even better things to come.

So hop on over to www.TurleyTalks.com and have a look around. Make sure to sign-up for our weekly Email Newsletter where you'll get lots of free giveaways, private Q&As, and tons of great content. Check out our YouTube channel (www.youtube.com/c/DrSteveTurley) where you'll understand current events in light of conservative trends to help you flourish in your personal and professional life. And of course, 'Like' us on Facebook and follow us on Twitter.

Thank you so much for your support and for your part in this cultural renewal.

About the Author

Steve Turley (PhD, Durham University) is an internationally recognized scholar, speaker, and classical guitarist. He is the author of *Awakening Wonder: A Classical Guide to Truth, Goodness, and Beauty* (Classical Academic Press) and *The Ritualized Revelation of the Messianic Age: Washings and Meals in Galatians and 1 Corinthians* (T&T Clark). Steve blogs on the church, society and culture, education, and the arts at TurleyTalks.com. He is a faculty member at Tall Oaks Classical School in Bear, DE, where he teaches Theology, Greek, and Rhetoric, and Professor of Fine Arts at Eastern University. Steve lectures at universities, conferences, and churches throughout the U.S. and abroad. His research and writings have appeared in such journals as *Christianity and Literature, Calvin Theological Journal, First Things, Touchstone*, and *The Chesterton Review*. He and his wife, Akiko, have four children and live in Newark, DE, where they together enjoy fishing, gardening, and watching *Duck Dynasty* marathons.

Made in the USA
San Bernardino, CA
26 November 2017